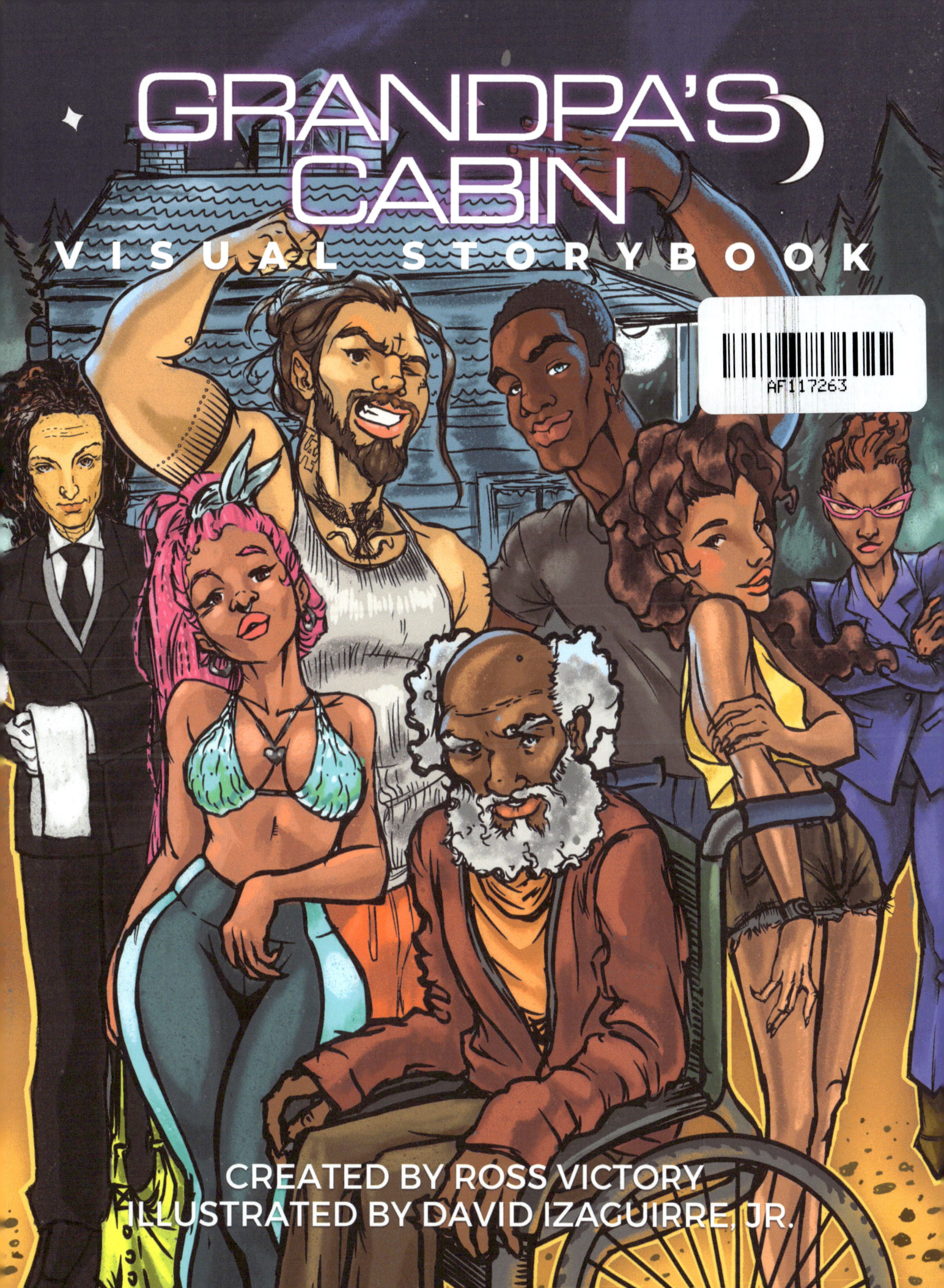

© COPYRIGHT 2023 BY J. ROSS VICTORY; ROSS VICTORY, VFTC UNIVERSE

ALL RIGHTS RESERVED.

NO PART OF THIS PUBLICATION MAY BE REPRODUCED, DISTRIBUTED, OR TRANSMITTED IN ANY FORM OR BY ANY MEANS, INCLUDING PHOTOCOPYING, RECORDING, OR OTHER ELECTRONIC OR MECHANICAL METHODS, WITHOUT THE PRIOR WRITTEN PERMISSION OF THE PUBLISHING AUTHOR, EXCEPT IN THE CASE OF BRIEF QUOTATIONS EMBODIED IN CRITICAL REVIEWS AND CERTAIN OTHER NONCOMMERCIAL USES PERMITTED SOLELY BY COPYRIGHT LAW. CONCEPTS AND CHARACTERS ARE THE COPYRIGHTED MATERIAL OF THE CREATOR. VIOLATION OF THE COPYRIGHT WILL BE PURSUED WITH AGGRESSIVE LEGAL ACTION.

CREATED & WRITTEN BY J. ROSS VICTORY
ROSSVICTORY.COM

COVER ILLUSTRATION BY DAVID IZAGUIRRE, JR.
IZYTHEREAL.COM

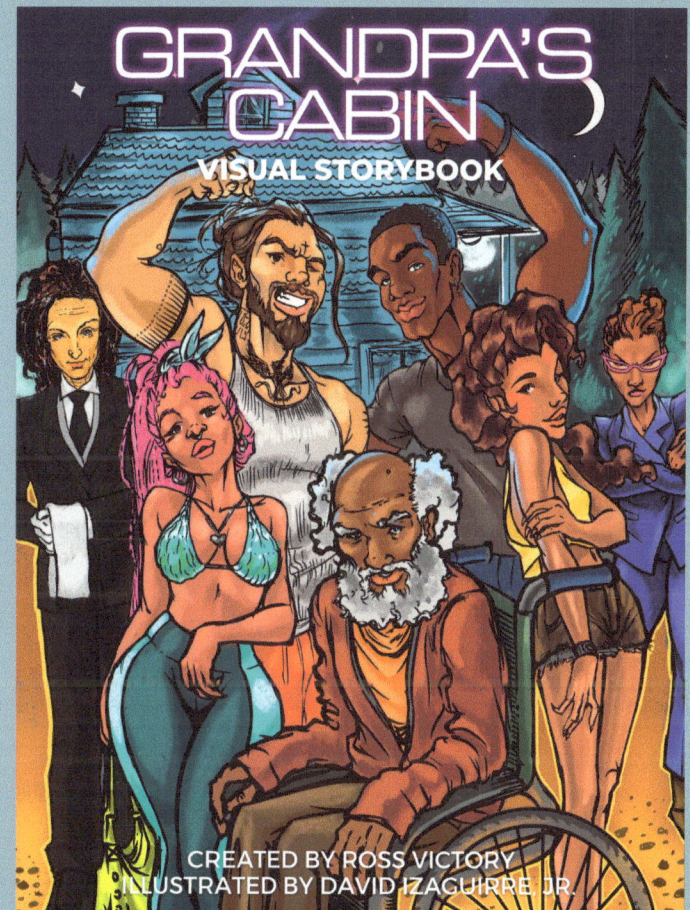

BOOK 1 SYNOPSIS

At eighty-four years old, widower and award-winning geneticist Bernie Crenshaw has reached the end of his life. Bernie gifts his only grandson, eighteen-year-old Inglewood high school senior Nova, his multimillion-dollar property located in Los Angeles' Hollywood hills.

Hours before his death, Bernie informs Nova that he did terrible deeds years ago. Bernie reveals that he never got caught because his freedom was contingent on an agreement he made with a "woman in the shadows" to keep the cabin in the family's bloodline. Nova promises his grandfather that he will never sell the property.

Years after Bernie's death, Nova hosts a wild twenty-first birthday party weekend filled with alcohol, music, and Only Fans web cameras. After a handful of eerie encounters in the surrounding Los Angeles forest, Nova's friends allege that grandpa's cabin is the burial ground for people who disappeared during their childhood.

The birthday weekend shifts from celebration to terror as the friends piece together that the man Nova knew as "Popsi" matches the profile of one of Los Angeles' most notorious wanted criminals—"L.A. Love Hunter."

Will Nova preserve the Crenshaw family's sadistic legacy, or will he choose the rare and valuable gift of friendship?

GRANDPA'S CABIN
in color

GRANDPA'S CABIN
in black and white

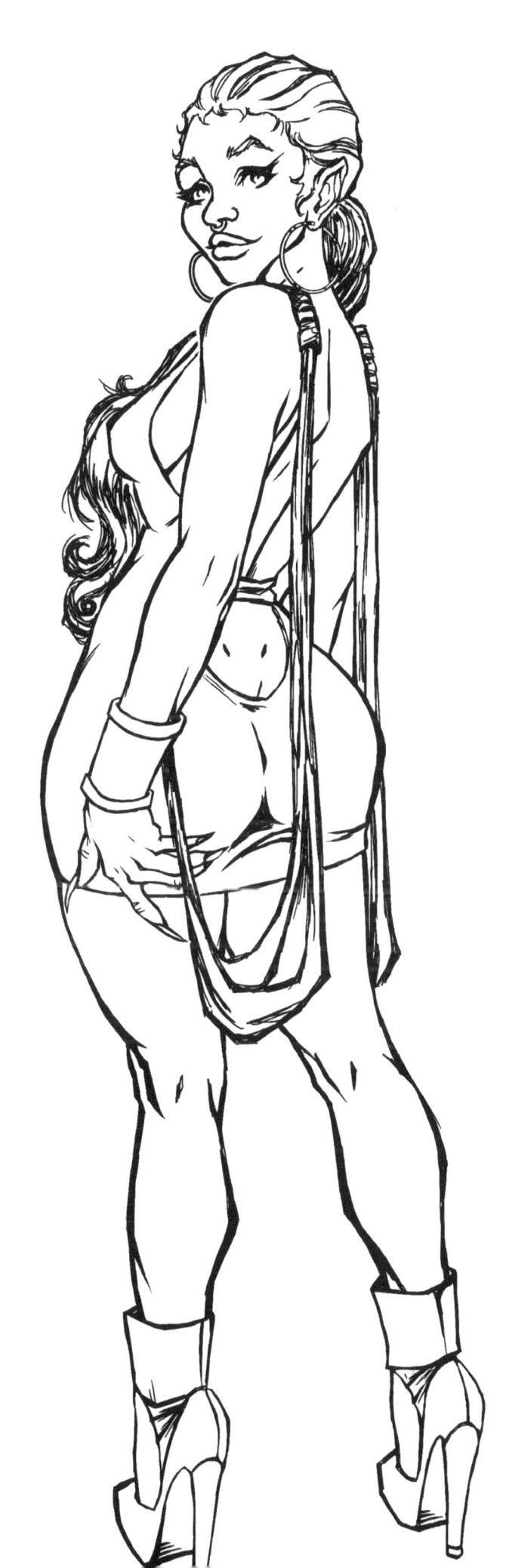

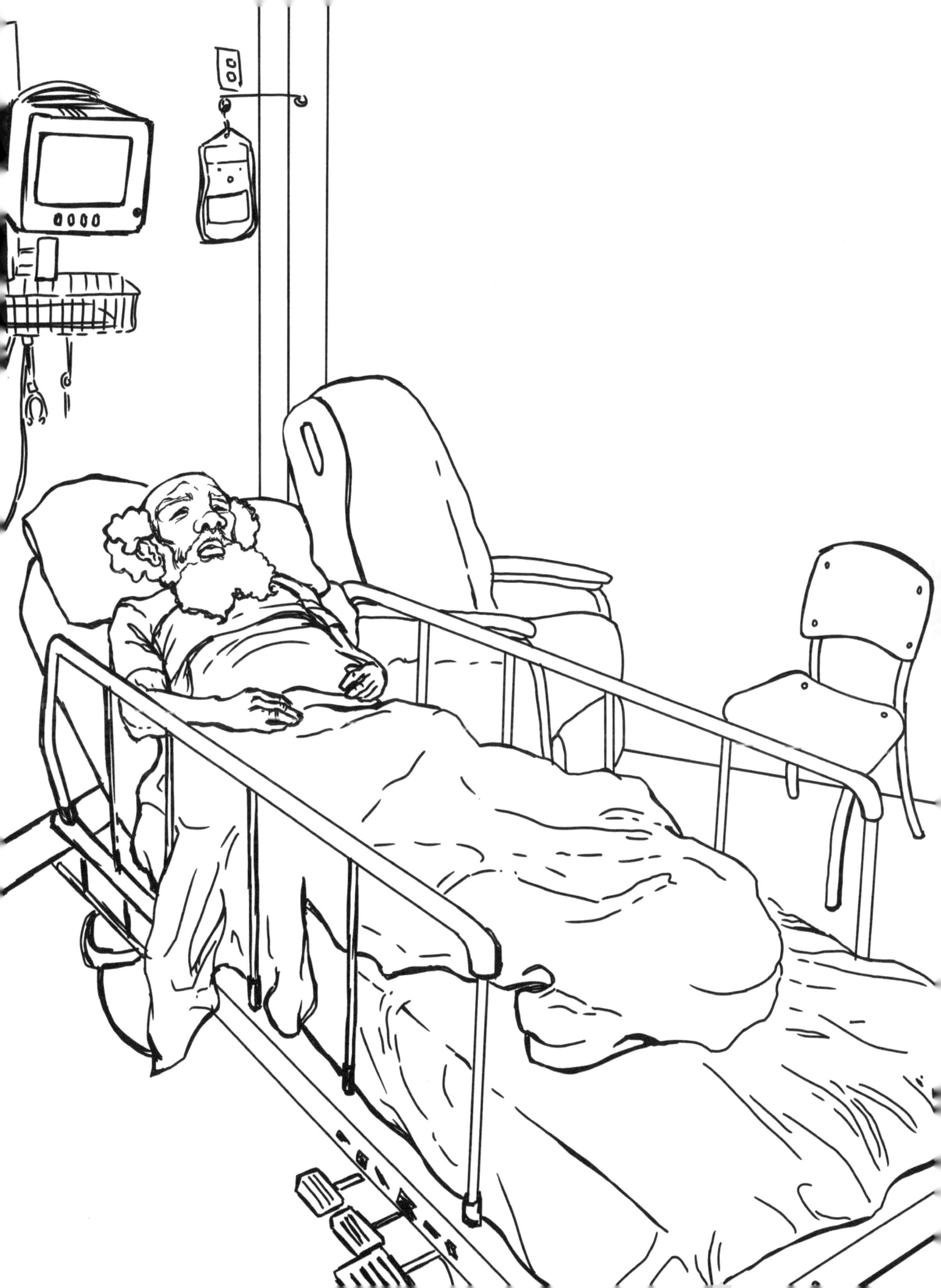

ABOUT THE CREATOR

Ross Victory is a singer/songwriter and award-winning author from Southern California.

After the loss of his father and brother, Ross dove into self-discovery, reigniting his childhood passion for writing and music production. Victory has dedicated his life to empowering the creative community while inspiring and entertaining listeners and readers. Victory provides a multi-format creative experience in Urban Adult Contemporary music and literature, with a focus on creative non-fiction and novellas.

Victory is best known for his father-son memoir, "Views from the Cockpit," and his brand,
"Books & Bangers."

GRANDPA'S CABIN

JOIN GRANDPA'S CABIN FAN COMMUNITY ON THE BAND APP

VISIT ROSSVICTORY.COM/GRANDPASCABIN

www.ingramcontent.com/pod-product-compliance
Lightning Source LLC
LaVergne TN
LVHW071658060526
838201LV00037B/378